Structural Wonders

Great Wall of China

Christine Webster

Published by Weigl Publishers Inc.
350 5th Avenue, Suite 3304, PMB 6G
New York, NY 10118-0069

Website: www.weigl.com

Library of Congress Cataloging-in-Publication Data

Webster, Christine.
  Great Wall / Christine Webster.
     p. cm. -- (Structural wonders)
  Includes index.
  ISBN 978-1-59036-723-0 (hard cover : alk. paper) -- ISBN 978-1-59036-724-7 (soft cover :
alk. paper)
  1. Great Wall of China (China)--Juvenile literature. 2. Military architecture--China--Juvenile
literature. I. Title.
  DS793.G67W43 2008
  623'.1951--dc22
                              2007012113

Printed in the United States of America
1 2 3 4 5 6 7 8 9 0 11 10 09 08 07

Photograph Credits
Every reasonable effort has been made to trace ownership and to obtain
permission to reprint copyright material. The publishers would be pleased
to have any errors or omissions brought to their attention so that they may
be corrected in subsequent printings.

All of the internet URLs given in the book were valid at the time of publication.
However, due to the dynamic nature of the Internet, some addresses may have
changed, or sites may have ceased to exist since publication. While the author
and publisher regret any inconvenience this may cause readers, no responsibility
for any such changes can be accepted by either the author or the publisher.

Project Coordinators: Heather C. Hudak, Heather Kissock
Design: Terry Paulhus

Contents

What is the Great Wall of China?

People have been building structures for centuries. A structure is any type of thing built by a human. Structures can be monuments, towers, houses, and even walls. Walls are upright structures built to surround something. They are used in playgrounds and houses, and they are used to fence yards. Walls have been built all over the world. In ancient history, walls often were used for protection.

The Great Wall of China was built for protection and to stop intruders from invading the area. It winds east to west through parts of China, traveling through deserts, around mountains, and to the sea. Construction of the Great Wall of China began more than 2,000 years ago. It took more than one thousand years to build. It is built from earth, stones, wood, and bricks.

The Great Wall is the longest wall ever built. Nobody knows the true length of the Great Wall. This is because it is so old. Some parts of the wall have been buried. Other parts have been destroyed. Historians can only measure what remains standing aboveground. It is about 3,948 miles (6,354 kilometers) long and stands up to 25 feet (7.6 meters) tall, with 40-foot (12-m) towers all along it.

Today, the Great Wall of China is used to attract people to visit the area. Millions of people visit this structure every year, making it one of the world's major tourist attractions. The Great Wall is one of the **Seven Wonders of the World**.

Quick Bites

- Many people have claimed that the Great Wall of China is visible from the Moon. This is not true.
- The Great Wall of China is made up of three walls. Each one was built during a different historical period in China.
- The highest point of the Great Wall is 4,265 feet (1,300 m) above sea level.

Building History

In the past, southern China was ruled by emperors. The land they ruled was rich with resources. People farmed the land, raising crops and sheep. The northern part of China, however, was home to a group of people called Mongolians. This area did not provide as many resources as the south. Mongolians had to trade for things they needed. Often, they were jealous of the abundance of the southern people. Sometimes, they would raid the area for things. This often led to fighting.

To stop the fighting, the emperor of China decided to build a huge wall. Qin Shi Huangdi was the first emperor of China. He ruled as emperor between the years 221 BC and 206 BC. The emperor thought that the wall would keep the Mongolians out of the south and stop them from raiding his area. He forced people that disagreed with his way of ruling to build the wall as part of their punishment.

In addition to the Great Wall, Qin Shi Huangdi ordered the construction of a national road system.

Qin Shi Huangdi had the wall built from packed earth and wooden frames. The labor was difficult. Workers had to haul dirt and stones hundreds of miles. They had little food or shelter, so many died. During Qin Shi Huangdi's **reign**, 1,500 miles (2,414 km) of the Great Wall were built.

A terracotta army surrounds the tomb of Emperor Qin Shi Huangdi. The tomb is located near Xian.

TIMELINE OF CONSTRUCTION

221 BC: China's first emperor, Qin Shi Huangdi, orders the construction of the Great Wall of China as a means of defense against the Mongolians.

AD 1200s: Ghenghis Khan, a Mongolian leader, breaks through the Great Wall.

1449: China is ruled by the Ming Dynasty. Building of the wall begins again.

1644: The Great Wall runs from Jiayuguan in the west, past the Gobi Desert, across the Yellow River, past Peking, which is now Beijing, and to Shanhaiguan in the east.

1644–1911: The wall is no longer needed for defense.

1984: Deng Xiaoping, leader of the People's Republic of China, orders that restoration efforts for the Great Wall be put in place.

1987: The Great Wall of China is made a **UNESCO World Heritage Site**. This recognition will help preserve and protect it.

Zhu Yuanzhang is buried at the Ming Xiaoling Mausoleum in Nanjing, China. Stone-carved animals guard the tomb.

The fighting between groups continued for many years. New emperors were defeated. Other emperors were replaced. The Mongolians continued to terrorize southern areas.

The Qin and Ming Dynasties did not call the structure the Great Wall of China. This name came from Europeans who visited the area.

Then, a new **dynasty**, called the Ming dynasty, came into power. It was led by a peasant farmer named Zhu Yuanzhang. Zhu Yuanzhang drove the Mongolians back to the grassy plains. Under his rule, the Ming dynasty continued building the Great Wall of China. The structure of the wall remained the same, but bricks were used instead of packed earth. Some tools were introduced, as well as better working conditions.

The wall continued to be built for hundreds of years, extending through the mountains, grassy plains, and deserts of China. By the 1600s, the Great Wall of China measured more than 3,728 miles (6,000 km), with more than 25,000 towers.

1

2

3

Structural Wonders

The best-preserved sections of the Great Wall are found near the city of Beijing.

Big Ideas

The Chinese wanted to protect themselves from invasions. They planned to build a wall around their entire territory. The wall would extend through all areas where enemy forces were known to enter. It would be high enough that it would be hard to scale. Towers would be placed along the wall so that soldiers could see great distances. If an enemy was spotted, smoke was sent up from the tower. Soldiers along the Great Wall would see the smoke signal and prepare for a fight. Enemies would be shot at with arrows.

During the Qin Dynasty, the Great Wall was built mostly from packed earth. Wooden frames shaped the earth wall. This type of the wall is found in the western part of China. The earth wall was strong—withstanding attacks of arrows and spears. Years later, during the Ming Dynasty, the wall was made much stronger. Gunpowder was now available. An earth wall would not stand up to cannons or **musket** attacks. Workers began using bricks and stones to construct the wall.

The Ming Dynasty had the best wall builders throughout the wall's construction. The portion of the wall built during this dynasty is in the eastern part of China. Most of the wall seen by tourists today was built during the Ming dynasty.

1) The Great Wall of China snakes through narrow passes and up steep hilltops. 2) Watch towers are found at regular intervals along the Great Wall. 3) From 1984 to 1985, Dong Yaohui walked along the standing parts of the Great Wall of China. His journey took 508 days. He was the first person to do this since 1949.

Profile:
Qin and Ming Dynasties

Throughout history, many emperors commanded the building of the Great Wall, but no one person is known to have designed the structure.

Although no architect was named, a man by the name of General Meng Tien oversaw more than half of the Great Wall's construction during the Qin Dynasty. General Meng Tien was the emperor's military commander.

Some believe that, under Meng Tien's supervision, approximately one million workers built a wall that stretched from the eastern part of the present-day Gansu Province to what is now known as Jilin Province. Meng Tien used natural resources and followed the shape of the land to construct about 1,500 miles (2,400 km) of the wall. Few parts of this original wall exist today. Over the next 2,000 years, different emperors used these methods to continue building the wall.

The Han Dynasty took control after the Qin Dynasty, and additional stretches of the wall were built. Following the Han Dynasty, the Northern Wei, Northern Qi, and Sui Dynasties also added to the wall.

ARCHITECTURAL STOPS ALONG THE GREAT WALL

Juyongguan Pass, Changping County, China
The Juyongguan **Pass** is found in the 11-mile (18-km) Guangou Valley. It is one of the three greatest passes along the Great Wall. This pass was built by the Ming Dynasty. It was once surrounded by lush flowers.

Shanghai Pass, Qinhaungdao, China
The Shanghai Pass is located at the eastern end of the Great Wall of China. For many years, it guarded a small pass between the northeast and central-east sections of China. The walls around the pass are 46 feet (14 m) high. Three sides are surrounded by a **moat**.

The Great Wall, as it stands today, was mostly built during the Ming Dynasty. In 1368, Zhu Yuanzhang ordered General Xu Da to begin rebuilding the wall. The Ming wall begins in Heilongjiang Province and stretches to Guansu. Additions and repairs were made to the wall until the Ming Dynasty fell to the Qing Dynasty in 1644.

The Ming Dynasty part of the wall passes nine cities, provinces, and autonomous, or independent, regions.

Jiayuguan Pass, Jiayuguan City, China
This is the first pass at the western end of the Great Wall. The pass is found between two hills. It is shaped like a trapezoid, which looks like a rectangle with a top that is shorter than the bottom. The Jiayuguan Pass covers an area of 360,591 square feet (33,500 square meters). It was built in 1372.

Mutianyu Great Wall, Huairou County, China
This part of the Great Wall connects the Juyongguan Pass from the west to the east. It is found about 43 miles (73 km) northeast of the city of Beijing and is one of the most well preserved parts of the wall. It measures 7,382 feet (2,250 m) long and has 22 watchtowers.

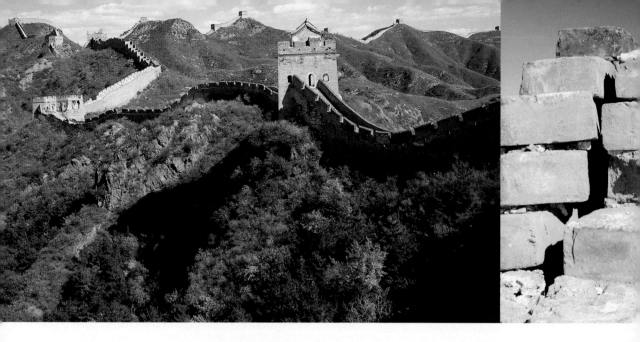

The Science Behind
the Building

The Great Wall needed to have specific features in order to hold back
intruders. It had to be sturdy, tall, and strong. For the wall to do its job,
it had to be indestructible.

Weight Loads

The architect knew that a wall like this carried a great deal of weight.
The designer had to create a structure that could handle strong forces and
heavy loads. A load is the total weight that an object can carry. In the case
of the Great Wall, this included materials and people. As well, the height
of the wall pushed weight down into the lower parts. This could cause the
wall to buckle or the center to bulge outward, ruining the shape of the
wall. For the Great Wall, packed earth was strong enough to withstand
the weight of the design. The Great Wall was designed so the bottom
was thicker than the top. As a result, the wall would not topple over.

Tamping Earth

When construction of the Great Wall began, workers used dirt as their
main material. They developed a way to use this material so that it would
remain strong when under attack. Workers used a method called *hang-tu*,

The Great Wall was built from materials such as dirt, rocks, and brick.

which means "beaten down earth." First, a frame for the wall, usually made from wood or bamboo sticks, was built. Then, workers carried baskets of earth and poured them into the wooden frame. With a rock or another tool, the earth was pounded into the ground. Packing earth like this removed air pockets. It allowed the dirt to form a strong compact layer that would not crumble. Each layer was only a few inches thick with dirt. Once the dirt was packed tightly, another layer was thrown on top. This method was repeated until the wall reached the required height. The slow process of packing dirt gradually built up the Great Wall of China layer by layer. Once the wall was the right height, the wooden frames were removed, and a new section was begun.

Types of Rocks

During the Ming Dynasty, the type of weapons being used changed. Cannons and muskets were a new form of weaponry. The wall had to be much stronger to withstand this new technology. The wall was built along mountainous areas, where rocks were abundant. The rocks were very strong—much stronger than earth—and would hold up against the new weaponry. Limestone, granite, white stones, and even marble are found throughout the Great Wall. All rocks are made up of two or more minerals. The measure of a mineral's toughness is called tenacity. Tenacity is how easily a rock will cut, bend, crumble, break, split, or change shape. Fracture refers to how it breaks once it has exceeded its maximum tenacity.

Web Link:
To find out more about rocks, visit www.rocksforkids.com/RFK/identification.html

Science and Technology

Today, computers are used to design walls, and factories make the materials. Cement mixers smooth concrete for easy use. Bulldozers clear the earth for the foundation. Cranes lift heavy bricks to the site. This technology was not always available. The workers who built the Great Wall had to use far more basic tools.

Tools and Supplies

In the early years of building the Great Wall, tools were limited. Wheelbarrows had not been designed. Bringing materials from one place to another required human effort. Thousands of workers were responsible for digging and carrying earth to the site. Often, they dug the dirt with their hands. Sometimes, they had simple shovels for digging. Woven baskets were used to carry the dirt to the site. Rocks, and sometimes wooden tools, were used to stomp the earth down. If resources were far from the site or the land was steep, workers formed an **assembly line**.

The stonecutter chipped rock into a rough rectangular shape to be used for the foundation, or the bottom of the wall.

They would line up along the wall, and the materials would be passed from one person to the next. Later in the wall's construction, rocks were used as building tools. Sometimes, rocks had to be cut from a mountain. A stonecutter would place a **chisel** on the rock. A chisel is a wedge-shaped, simple machine. A wedge is used to push things apart by converting motion on one direction into a splitting motion at the other end. The splitting occurs at right angles to the blade. As the stonecutter pounded a **mallet** against the chisel, the rock would chip away.

Ladders and Ramps

Reaching tall heights was a challenge during the construction of the Great Wall. Ramps of packed earth allowed workers to reach higher areas.

Wheelbarrows could be filled with materials and pushed up a ramp to a higher location.

A ramp is a type of simple machine called an inclined plane. A plane is a flat surface. When it is slanted, or inclined, at an angle other than a right angle, it can help move objects across distances. Using a relatively small force, one can move a large resistance, such as a rock. Early versions of the ladder were also used to reach tall heights. These were made of wooden bamboo sticks that were tied together with rope. By the time of the Ming Dynasty, wheelbarrows had been introduced. Wheelbarrows use a wheel and axle to move objects across distances. The wheel turns the axle. An object can be placed on top of the axle to move it more easily.

Pulley Systems

Hoisting heavy rocks and bricks introduced another obstacle. When the materials were too heavy for a human to lift, a rope pulley system had to be used. A pulley uses a wheel and a rope. The wheel has a groove along the edge where the rope sits. Baskets could be tied to the ropes and materials placed inside. By pulling on the rope, the wheel would turn. This action moved the basket up toward the pulley. This method allowed workers to transport heavy materials to greater heights.

Computer-Aided Design

Architects are trained professionals who work with clients to design structures. Before anything is built, they make detailed drawings or models. These plans are important tools that help people visualize what the structure will look like. A blueprint is a detailed diagram that shows where all the parts of the structure will be placed. Walls, doors, windows, plumbing, electrical wiring, and other details are mapped out on the blueprint. Blueprints act as a guide for engineers and builders during construction.

For centuries, architects and builders worked without the aid of computers. Sketches and blueprints were drawn by hand. Highly skilled drafters would draw very technical designs. Today, this process is done using computers and sophisticated software programs. Architects use CAD, or computer-aided design, throughout the design process. Early CAD systems used computers to draft building plans. Today's computer programs can do much more. They can build three-dimensional models and computer simulations of how a building will look. They can also calculate the effects of different physical forces on the structure. Using CAD, today's architects can build more complex structures at lower cost and in less time.

Computer-aided design programs have been used since the 1960s.

Eye on Design
Remote Sensing Technology

Previous attempts have been made to measure the Great Wall. However, parts of the wall have been discovered as recently as 2002. Remote sensing may help determine if other parts are still uncovered.

The exact length of the Great Wall of China is unknown. Parts have fallen down, and some of the wall has been buried. Scientists have decided to remeasure the Great Wall using remote sensing technology (RST).

Remote sensing technology gathers information from a distance without actually coming into contact with the object being measured. It uses data from aerial and ground satellites. RST detects and measures different **radiation** wavelengths that are emitted or reflected from an object. Then, it puts the information into a computer. The computer analyzes the data and draws up an accurate measurement.

Previously, the Great Wall was measured onsite. Today, remote sensing technology will provide accurate measurements, and even photographs, of the remaining Great Wall.

MEASURING THE GREAT WALL OF CHINA

Location
The Great Wall is located along China's northern border.

Length
Some estimates suggest that the wall is 3,948 miles (6,354 km) long.

Wall Size
- Between 15 to 25 feet (4.6 to 7.6 m) high
- 15 to 30 feet (4.6 to 9.1 m) wide at the base
- 9 to 12 feet (2.7 to 3.7 m) wide at the top

Other Interesting Facts
- Archaeologists found two chessboards on the Great Wall, estimated to be at least 700 years old. They were probably used by soldiers to pass the time.
- Holes can be found along the wall. These holes are about 1 foot (0.3 m) tall and 9 inches (23 cm) wide. They were used to aim arrows before shooting them out toward the enemy.

Environmental Viewpoint

Due to the Great Wall's extreme age, it needs to be preserved. Parts of the Great Wall have collapsed. Some parts are going to collapse. Other parts may disappear forever unless action is taken to ensure it lasts for future generations. In fact, only 20 percent of the entire wall is considered to be in decent shape. Thirty percent is ruined, and the rest is gone permanently.

The wall is deteriorating from **weathering**, **erosion**, humans, and construction. Weathering, such as wind and rain, has worn parts of the wall away. Plants and roots have grown inside cracks, causing them to widen. This breaks the brick down further. Exhaust fumes from vehicles are ruining the bricks as well, causing them to erode. Large amounts of litter are left along the walkway from tourists. This damages the environment that supports the wall.

About 10 million people visit the Great Wall each year. This causes damage to the wall. Some people have stolen bricks from the wall. They use them for building their homes. Some parts of the wall have been demolished by construction crews that have destroyed sections for their own use. People have drawn graffiti on some parts of the wall. They have also scratched markings into the brick with knives or hairpins.

Preserving a structure as expansive as the Great Wall takes the dedicated effort of many people.

In 2003, a local municipal government created a law. This law stated that all people are obliged to help protect the Great Wall. This will help protect it and preserve it for thousands of years. The Great Wall was also listed as a UNESCO World Heritage Site in 1987. World Heritage Sites are selected for their cultural or natural importance. They are protected and preserved.

PRESERVATION

In 2003, a conservation area was opened to help preserve the Great Wall and its surrounding environment. The area is called the International Friendship Forest.

The forest is located at the foot of the Great Wall of China at the Badaling gate in the western area. The idea behind this area is to restore the natural forest found here.

The International Friendship Forest is a 40-acre (16-hectare) area used for restoring the **ecology** to what it once was. Native trees and plants have been replanted in order to do this.

At this park, visitors can walk along trails and view the Great Wall. Signs along the trails have been added to educate people about the story of the park. They also tell the story behind the building of this part of the Great Wall. With more projects like these, the Great Wall of China will be protected for centuries.

Construction Careers

Building the Great Wall of China took an enormous number of people. During the Qin Dynasty, many people were ordered to work on the wall. Farmers were ordered off their land and onto a construction crew. Prisoners were taken out of prison to work on the wall. The working conditions during this time were harsh. Camps were made along the wall. The daily meal consisted of a bowl of rice and cooked cabbage. Rain, snow, and wind blew around the workers. The workers hauled baskets of earth and pounded the dirt with rocks, sometimes for sixteen hours a day. A million people died and were buried in trenches along the wall. Qin ordered the wives of the men who died to work on the wall.

During the Ming Dynasty, there was a need for skilled workers. The wall had to be more precise. This called for the need of quarry workers, laborers, and brick makers, or masons.

Quarry Workers

Quarry workers cut stones from nearby quarries. They used metal chisels and hammers to shape the block. The heavy rock was then loaded into carts and, with pulleys, was delivered to the site. Today, quarry workers use drilling machines and explosives to break up rock. Many quarry sites are located in rural areas, so workers must travel to work. Quarry work is dirty, dusty, and noisy. It takes place outdoors in all types of weather conditions.

Masons

The emperors of the Ming Dynasty knew the Great Wall needed to be sturdy. On its own, dirt was not strong enough to keep out intruders. To solve this problem, the Ming emperor consulted brick makers. Brick makers in ancient China made bricks from the materials on hand, such as clay or dirt. The dirt was mixed with water and cooked hard in a **kiln**. The mixture of clay or dirt and water was then put into wooden molds. The molds helped to shape the bricks and make sure that each brick was the same size. The molds were then put into the kiln and cooked. Once cooled, the bricks were removed from the molds and were ready to use on the wall. Today, masons continue to work on buildings. They shape bricks and stones and lay them in place.

Laborers

Laborers made up the majority of workers on the Great Wall. They were responsible for doing many tasks. They filled baskets with dirt and carried heavy rocks. They hoisted wheelbarrows full of ready-made bricks to the site. Laborers continue to play an important role in construction. They perform many jobs, including cleaning sites, building concrete forms, loading materials, and operating equipment. Some jobs require special training, while others can be done without experience. However, laborers should be physically fit to do most jobs.

Web Link:
To find out more about masonry, visit www.masonrysociety.org.

Notable Structures

In China, people have been building walls for thousands of years. Some surround houses and settlements. Others act as political borders between regions. Between 403 and 221 BC, many states fought for control of much of the land that is now China. People from some of these states, such as Qin, Yen, and Zhao, pounded earth to build walls along their territories.

The Forbidden City

Built: 1406 to 1420

Location: Beijing, China

Design: Emperor Young Le

Description: Today, this city is called the Palace Museum. It was built during the Ming Dynasty. The palace is surrounded by a wall that stands 33 feet (10 m) high and a moat. The city has more than 800 buildings. People could not enter the palace without the emperor's permission. This is where the idea of the "forbidden" city came.

Temple of Heaven

Built: 1420

Location: Beijing, China

Design: Ming and Qing Dynasties

Description: This temple is used for worship. It covers 1.05 square miles (2.73 square kilometers) of land. The temple is made up of three main structures—the Earthly Mount, the House of Heavenly Lord, and the Hall for Prayer for Good Harvests. Each structure was used for prayer.

The Great Wall is one of the best-known structures in the world. However, walls are just one example of Chinese structures. Many other ancient Chinese buildings exist in Beijing and other parts of the country.

Ming Tombs

Built: 1368 to 1644

Location: near Beijing, China

Design: Built for 13 emperors of the Ming Dynasty

Description: These tombs were originally built for Emperor Zhudi and his wives, but they now house 12 other emperors. The main building of this tomb is 21,054 square feet (1,956 square meters). Gold bricks line the floor. Two tombs are open for public viewing. The other 11 tombs are not.

Jokhang Temple

Built: 647

Location: Lhasa, Tibet, China

Design: King Songtsen Gampo

Description: This **Buddhist** temple is one of China's most popular tourist attractions. It covers an area of more than 269,098 square feet (25,000 sq m). Hundreds of **pilgrims** visit here daily. They have been coming to the Jokhang Temple for thousands of years.

Walls Around the World

China is not the only country that has built walls. Walls have been constructed all over the world for thousands of years. This map shows the location and length of some of the world's best-known walls.

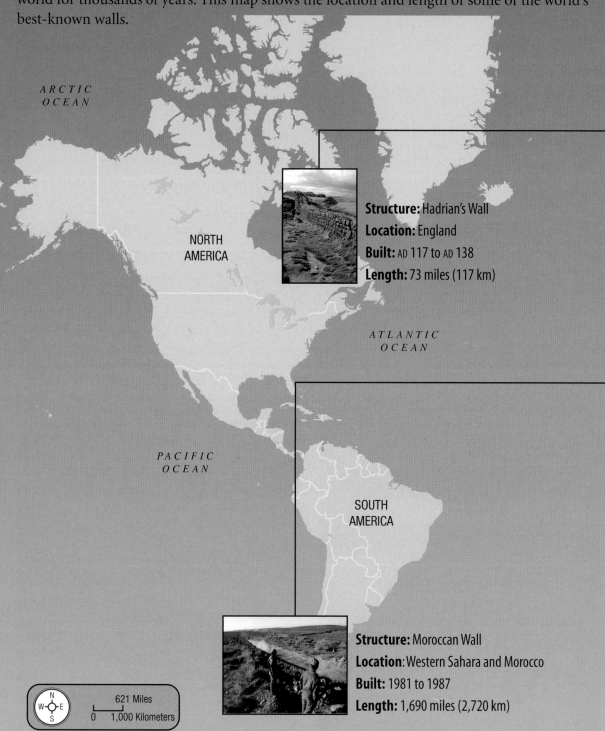

ARCTIC
OCEAN

NORTH
AMERICA

Structure: Hadrian's Wall
Location: England
Built: AD 117 to AD 138
Length: 73 miles (117 km)

ATLANTIC
OCEAN

PACIFIC
OCEAN

SOUTH
AMERICA

Structure: Moroccan Wall
Location: Western Sahara and Morocco
Built: 1981 to 1987
Length: 1,690 miles (2,720 km)

621 Miles

0   1,000 Kilometers

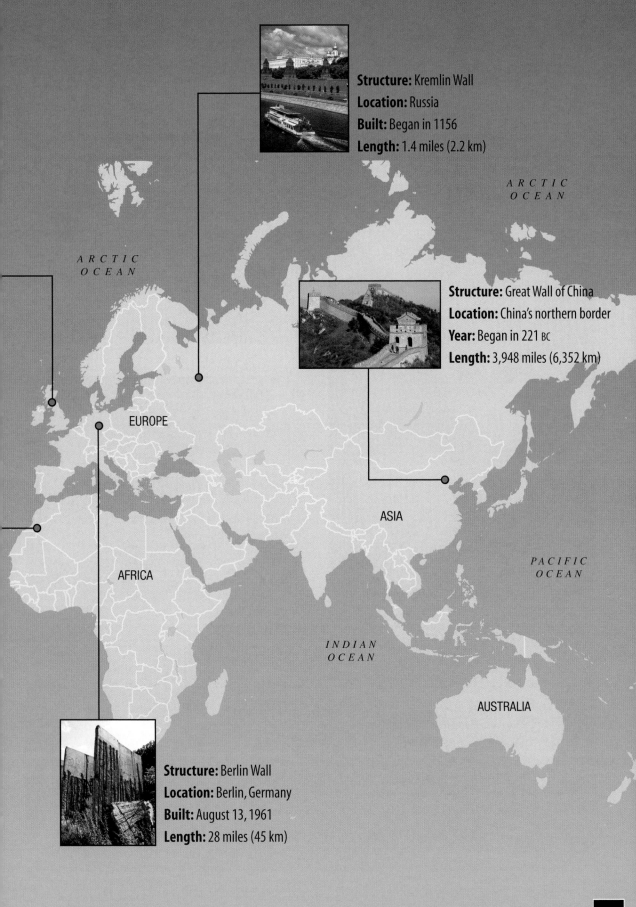

Structure: Kremlin Wall
Location: Russia
Built: Began in 1156
Length: 1.4 miles (2.2 km)

ARCTIC
OCEAN

ARCTIC
OCEAN

Structure: Great Wall of China
Location: China's northern border
Year: Began in 221 BC
Length: 3,948 miles (6,352 km)

EUROPE

ASIA

PACIFIC
OCEAN

AFRICA

INDIAN
OCEAN

AUSTRALIA

Structure: Berlin Wall
Location: Berlin, Germany
Built: August 13, 1961
Length: 28 miles (45 km)

Quiz

Q What tools did ancient Chinese workers use to build the Great Wall?

A Ancient Chinese workers cleared land with their hands or shovels and lifted things using ladders, pulleys, or ramps.

Q How does a pulley system work?

A A rope is seated along the groove of a wheel. By pulling the rope along the wheel, an item can be moved along easily.

Q Explain the process of making bricks.

A Clay or water and dirt are mixed together. The mixture is poured into wooden molds. Then, it is baked in a kiln until it is hard.

Q Name two reasons earth was pounded after it was piled in the wooden frame.

A Earth was pounded to remove air pockets. This prevented it from crumbling later on. Packing the earth also made it strong.

Make a Sweet Great Wall

Bricks are often used to build structures. Try this activity to build your own Great Wall.

Materials
- sugar cubes
- white glue
- 12 by 4 inch (30 by 10 cm) piece of wood

Instructions

1. Glue one row of sugar cubes onto the long, flat side of the wood.

2. On the other side, glue another row so there are two lines. This will make up the edges of the two walls.

3. Begin gluing another row of sugar cubes on top of the first two rows. Be sure that the center of each sugar cube in the second row is placed evenly over both edges of the two sugar cubes beneath.

4. Continue in this pattern until you have two tall walls.

Further Research

You can find more information on the the Great Wall of China, China, and the world's best-known structures at your local library or on the Internet.

Websites

For more information about the Great Wall of China, visit www.thegreatwall.com.cn/en

Read about China at www.cnto.org/aboutchina.asp

To take a virtual tour of the Great Wall, visit www.thechinaguide.com/great_wall_of_china/index.html

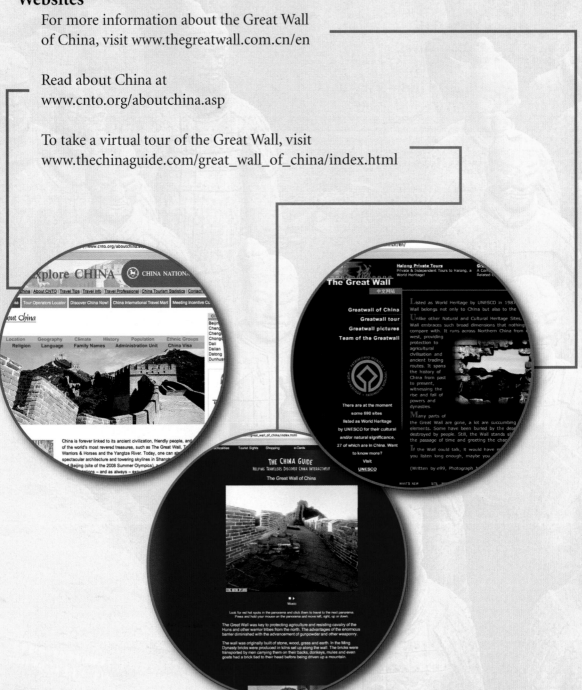

Glossary

assembly line: a sequence of machines, tools, and workers arranged so that, at each stage, a further process is carried out

Buddhist: a person who follows the teachings of Buddha

chisel: a hand tool consisting of a flat steel blade with a handle

dynasty: a sequence of rulers from the same family

ecology: the study of relationships between living organisms and their environment

erosion: the wearing away of rocks, soil, etc., by the action of water, ice, or wind

kiln: large oven for burning, drying, or processing something

mallet: a tool resembling a hammer

moat: a wide, water-filled ditch surrounding a fortified place

mortar: a mixture used as a bond between bricks or stones

musket: a gun

pass: a route through a range of mountains where there is a gap between peaks

pilgrims: people who journey to a sacred place to worship

radiation: the transfer of radiant energy as electromagnetic waves

reign: the period when an emperor rules the land

Seven Wonders of the World: the seven structures considered by scholars to be the most wondrous of the world

UNESCO World Heritage Site: a site designated by the United Nations to be of great cultural worth to the world and in need of protection

weathering: the breaking down of rocks by the action of rain, snow, etc.

Index